Sorgmantel

Sorgmantel

Richard Fenton Sederstrom

Published by the Jackpine Writers' Bloc, Inc.

Copyright © 2018 Richard Fenton Sederstrom
All rights reserved
ISBN: 978-1-928690-39-9
Published in the United States of America

Published by the Jackpine Writers' Bloc, Inc.
Edited by Sharon Harris
Layout and cover design by Tarah L. Wolff

Also by Richard Fenton Sederstrom

Fall Pictures on an Autumn Road

Disordinary Light

Folly: A Book of Last Summers

Eumaeus Tends

Selenity Book Four

Acknowledgments

The poet gratefully acknowledges the following magazines as the original publishers of the following poems:

The Blue Guitar Magazine: "Autumn Early Light in Chauvet," "*Cathartes aura in Opere et Veritate,*" "Common Icons of New England," "Fenton's Lucretius," "Frail Sounds," "Sorgmantel."

Dissident Voice: "Among the Water Lilies."

Unstrung: "Breathing Under Water," parts 1 and 2, "en-Chantment," "Mason Jar," "The Room Where We Three Pass."

"War Games: Demodocus Deposes from a Rocky Hill in Arcadia" appeared in the poet's *Eumaeus Tends,* in a slightly different form.

Cover: *Nymphalis antiopa,* from *The Papilios of Great Britain*, by William Lewin, London, 1795.

Acknowledgments

My conversations with other members of my family, especially Hugh Fenton and Francis Fenton, made the core of this book possible, and Loren Sederstrom and I seem to be listening to one another, for now.

*

For their generous and patient reading and unstinting criticism, that I have listened to more than my responses might indicate, my thanks to Alan Johnson, Randel Helms, and Arthur Colby, scholars, guides, and friends.

*

I owe a great debt of gratitude to Rebecca Dyer, editor of *The Blue Guitar Magazine* and *Unstrung*, for her unreserved support of my experiments and eccentricities for almost a decade now.

*

And now it is the sixth occasion to thank Sharon Harris and Tarah L. Wolff for their continuing forbearance, their unremitting care for my work and for their artistry as they continue to make sure that my books are blunder-free and attractive way beyond my ken and skill.

Dedication

As always, this book is for Carol, my love, my dearest companion and tender guide of my senses, and for Nick Salerno, my oldest friend, now gone, who remains my teacher, my conscience, and my second dearest critic.

And for my children, my grandchildren, and great-grandchildren. I wish you each a peaceful and fulfilling life. I fear for you and for my wishes.

Contents

- 1   I. Mourning Cloak I
- 3   Lithopsyche
- 6   Autumn Early Light at Chauvet
- 8   Cathartes aura in Opere et Veritate
- 10   Breathing under Water 1
- 13   Breathing under Water 2
- 16   Among the Water Lilies

- 17   II. Frail Sounds
- 19   War Games: Demodocus Deposes from a Rocky Hill in Arcadia
- 22   Frail Sounds
- 31   Poem in Three Places at Once
- 34   In Silence
- 36   We Shall See in Repair the Roads to Our Future

- 39   III. Lyric, Epic, Hearth
- 41   en-Chant-ment
- 42   Lyric/Epic
- 47   Epic/Hearth
- 50   Hearth/Lyric

- 55   IV. Verse and Reversion
- 57   The Room Where We Three Pass
- 59   Mason Jar
- 61   Fenton's Lucretius

- 77   V. Mourning Cloak II
- 79   Sorgmantel
- 81   Common Icons of New England
- 87   Transparencies
- 90   After Time After

- 93   *Notes*

The eccentricity that propels this sequence is the poet's: his selenity about finding the source, the compelling *da-sein*—the primal hearth: that cave.

Poetry is the impulse that preceded the actual production of imagined language. Some ancient time ago, a voice at the hearth uttered a meaningful sound divorced of utility, and she and someone else suddenly lost breath for a moment and were sent some-no-where entirely new and momently sublime.

But it was in the vocal response, carrying the first sound even further, that the urge to create something new in words alone, for no practical and identifiable purpose—song: poetry—really happened. It still doesn't happen very often; it doesn't last long, but it happens, and it recurs. These poems are *re*-currences.

The unintentional result of the experiment is that these poems have evolved into a prelude to an elegy that could neither be uttered nor recur: we live in the first era of human history when we are fatally able to produce "the fire next time." It would be pleasant, we might conclude, if we found a way not to.

To the end of that discovery, these poems are also *oc*-currences intended to recur in your creative conversation.

Sorgmantel

Språket rör sig över sina möjligheters
                komplexa yta
Drar sig sedan tillbaka
Efter en kort
fullbordan i

I. Mourning Cloak I

Lithopsyche

The genesis of the poem is the simple science.
The man with the bent finger sloshes chemicals
around in a bowl, sorts molecules about
until he has created the color that will become

the art of his hand, the signature as we may
—inadequately—see it. The color in the solution
will bond to the rock wall and create the texture
of our stunned and primitive reaction to the bison

on the wall, the entrance for our flight into
the vast and stupefying texture of our spinning
imaginations. Ideas, *Prolepses* and *clinamena*, nudge
the atoms. The fine and dangerous mind of Lucretius:

the fine and dangerous mind that is Life.
*

Chrysalis, Imago: molecules: the same molecules?
or a more—or less—imaginative group—of What?
Or . . . It is no mystery, if we chance to read from
the molecule's sempi-rational point of view.

What memory does Imago have of its discarded Larva?
Or, may each travel through a dimension of its own,
a cellular premonition—force of its own Imago,
psyche of the cosmos of its future?
*

Is Chrysalis a repository of memory?
Is Chrysalis a cleansing of memory? Both?

Lucretius will choose to agree, I think,
that the egg itself is a repository of atomic memory,
the fall and swerve of atoms moving through
creation to make somehow the music of ovum.
            *

Larva is the ghost, the mask. Disguising what?
Larva is a munching factory of energies.
Persona dies and rises to become Imago.
Persona of the image, the ghost

of the mask, persona of personae
multiplies in energies to swerve back
to the concatenation of atoms, dreams
its chemical re-creation of re-creations

poema composed of ghosts of ghosts
almost real each incarnaton, composed
finally into the persona of an appetite living
only to eat and die and flutter into its

Imago, a sacred influence of fluid behaviors:
The me?   O!   The Us.
The models and patterns of our ideas;
the Us of how many novel generations?
            *

Sorgmantel

Genetic gravitation toward cellular reconstruction—
its second self in a new being, self-created, undetermined,
a photon of awareness into our shared mortal Other:

ii

    something like a soul
registered in a lithic photograph.

Autumn Early Light at Chauvet

Retire to the cave.
Try to match the flicker of mortal torch
to the flicker of the torch behind your eyes.

See. Touch what scares you so badly.
Or since you cannot know
choose an image.

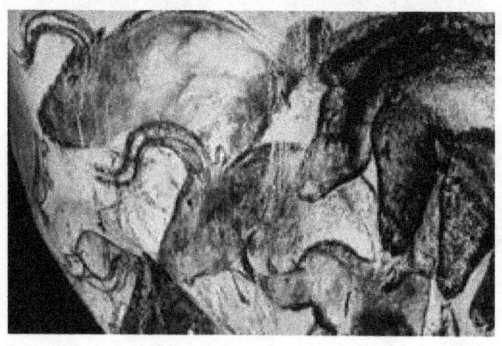

That aurochs.
Her honed horns. Her
unendurable force of

Sorgmantel

muscle, hoof, neck muscles rigid
against her spine's angry bone. Projectile of thunder.
It is the cave, the beast, and inside it all

what you may perceive as you—and death. Elect
to jump somewhere in the confines
of the darkness and binding rock.

Or elect to face the animal and die.
7017[iii] was a bad year, run of seasons,
an election of fears you are well evolved from.

7018 may be a better year. Light up
the cave then and let shine out the new. The rising
fire of your torch ignites the eye of the aurochs

and she elects to move.

Cathartes aura in Opere et Veritate
   for David Chorlton

1
Squat junipers dot valley and mountainside
in the desert view from David's photo.

Juniper boughs, cool green on the dexter side of the landscape.
Some tree, in shadow, arrests a partial symmetry on the
            sinister.

Symmetry is a human craving, desperate and consoling.
Below notice to the vulture

whose consolation is to perch atop the skeleton
of another juniper, the human camera's

2
middle focus.
A purification.

It is desert.
Desert translates light to clean air and arid breeze.

3
That sere, petrified gray branch will support the vulture
and generations of vultures to come.

The vulture's bland attention purports a view
that two beings understand the fortunate life of the vulture.

            Sorgmantel

One is the photographer
who frames the subtle asymmetric wonder of the vulture's
> world.

The other is the vulture, who sees and tastes that world
and its symmetric Stygian counter-world: like as not the same
> place.

4
Ah, but one other being too—an obfuscated interlocutor:
the poet: vulture's dys-symmetric confidante.

Breathing Under Water 1
preceding a theme by Gunnar Ekelöf

Lying on your back,
warming chill just under the surface of the brook
and clinging to enough bankside reediness
to be sure that this will be a respite—
and not a trip but a sojourn,
time for rest and contemplation—

you sink just far enough under
that what you see above
is the same dreamscape you see
when you peer through
the ancient window,
the ghost-lens original glass
at the north end of your family house.

Yes, like that.
A cosmic kaleidoscope
prism of ripples.
And yes
I hear you repeat that you can't.
Can't breathe.
You'll drown.

And I respond that I agree perfectly
but go ahead and do it anyway
just like last time

Sorgmantel

and the time before that.

Don't you remember?
Ah.

Not possible of course.
Remember anyway.
Breathe anyway.
                    *

Sticks float by, even branches.
They have floated by since before
the moon chose to evolve for you
from a child's night-mare
ghastly with teeth.
Sticks bump against rocks and growth.
They have since before those rocks were sucked round

and spat out by the destructive and creative glacier
who drifted enormously by
millennia before the trees
sprouted and grew to drop sticks and branches
to float in our common direction,
poke and pique our idle intention.
                    *

Lie in the stream.
Look skyward, moonward.
Consider.

What the glacier cannot remember,
what the moon *will not* remember,
you and the water above you will remember
and together tend the flow of stream and memory.

Breathe together—
you, the moon, the kaleidoscope of sky.

Sorgmantel

Breathing Under Water 2
avoiding the theme by Gunnar Ekelöf

Now you remember
and you can see what rises above you.
But what?

Let us agree that
above us a blue heron haunts the brook.
Whatever neighbor the heron does not bother to haunt
cannot be aware of the condition *haunted*
and so becomes anyway
its haunted and haunting prey:

frogs, minnows,
baby birds fallen from their nest and drifting
downstream
toward what none of them can possibly recognize
as beak, as weapon,
as poniard-pointed spring-locked machine,
as what must also be *because*

we are down here under
watching but also unavailable
to the information I supplied us with just now that we,
you and I and whomever you and I can imagine—

only because the instant of mention is the object—
that we also fail to recognize

what stalks above as what drives
below in its appetite to digest
what it spears and swallows:

Us!
The heron having fed to such satiety as it ever can—
the frogs, the minnows,
the struggling baby bird,

the us—
flies away to digest us
or to share us with its own progeny
giving us another chance at particulate immortality,
some caloric value.
Molecular virtue.

And those survivors who are left behind
still lying in the caressing stream
and who have determined not to suffer
what may have and *didn't* happen to us?

We know as well as they that we *choose* to flow
with assembling remnants
in a stream of evolving possibilities,
eons of nothing but sacred wedded particularities.

Sorgmantel

Among the Water Lilies

1

A crane tips her delicate beak down
down among the water lilies. Green
pads sport yellow white pink buds
like tea-time confections.

And blossoms unfolded.
Lotus morsels offer sweet peace
to the crane among them
and the frogs minnows crayfish

she entertains while they all
sleep their idyllic way into her welcoming gullet.
The crane lifts the shine of fine beak
from out the first dream: lotus Eden.

She raises her neck high
to reach even above late summer cattails
and strains her irongray loop of neck

2

to crane immense girders and bales of rebar

lordly above the uncontrolled slather
of draining nature, green yellow white pink.
Adjusts to the rightangle of monument aborning,
capital perfection of human genius.

3
Motored along by the refined primordium,
steered by the steady arm of public policy,

she lifts incendiary iron bars like ignorant keys
into a judgment of electric sky.

Sorgmantel

II. Frail Sounds

War Games: Demodocus Deposes from a Rocky Hill in Arcadia

... But still ... The old gods
were dependable. They were even comforting
in their horrifying playfulness,
their glorious selenity.

An island explodes as we have heard islands have done.
A great ship stands with its stone crew
as an obsidian monument to angry water games.
Phaeacia bound by insurmountable cliffs.

We declare the catastrophe an act of the gods
or one of them or the result of a spat between two of them
or an all-out war amongst them.
Or a lunatic act of lordly revenge.

Spite writ cosmic on some poor lubber after he's been fooled
into holding his head too high above the sheepfold.

Nobody blamed the gods for any of this, or not much.
The gods did what gods do.
Our part wasn't to question.
Our part was to tell the story in a manner to make grander the
        Grand.

Make something like wisdom out of Athena's Night-taloned
        bitchiness.
Make catastrophe of her diddling Odysseus.
Goddess of War and Wisdom?
Athens is well endowed with her name and her duplicity

and her step-child, Plato.

Understand that none of the gods paid attention to subtlety
or a well-turned metaphor, especially if we were to invent
and re-invent as we sung along
and did it fast.

So. Thera gets blown to dust, ash, and flecks of drifting bone.
A drying blood spot here and there.
We don't need to question.
The poet invents, grabs up his lyre and sings, and sings.

It was never our part
to worry about the general state of morality
and worry over what gods and heroes might have done
that we had better watch ourselves about—
or share the guilt with fellow sinners
or share any guilt, or sin.

Our dying was never so petty—
even the lowly among us, like poets.
Ours was to find a place in the cosmos of stories to fit it all in
and then some.

It's still the story that counts. Always.
Even for those of us who choose to stay in the rock-strewn
                    outlands
above Tempe or Dorset or far Wessex
munching the simple joys of jujubes and popcorn,
the penny groundlings and our subterranean genius.

Sorgmantel

We vagabond wag-tongues are the interlocutors
between the gods and their mortal masters.
To remain human without story
is to resign our souls to politics and hapless faith.

Frail Sounds

*To enjoy living in the Anthropocene is to
take refuge in the promise of immortality.
Nevertheless, we are Geology.*

1. February 2017

Water drops drop drop blink
into this tiny garden pond,
discrete, particular, fat-round,
enduring robust for a couple of feet—
their lives eternal for bright seconds
a tiny system of tiny mortal planets.

Their sun a sound: Blink
blink
blink
blink—
geologic time zones balance stasis with evolution.
Each blink a new Earth dissolving.
    *

Winter winking at me this morning,
this afternoon it will be spring again.
We will open all the windows of our world
into our world
and the grandmother fragrance of sweet acacia
will glimmer purplishly into the bedroom.

Sorgmantel

Outside under the tree
is a closer gesture of fragrance—
my grandmother's fragrance—
arms outspread sideways, palms up.
It is acceptance. It is Nature's submission
to the fleeting joy of our senses.
*

Combat helicopters range overhead.
The omnivorous grace
of military aggression. Earnest-eyed
Powers and Thrones drone,
hunting hard for something
to protect their feeble nation from.
*

You cannot help it, Richard,
accepting.
You have taken politics outside with you.
Your fists had been anchored
and you failed
to bother to switch off the television.

Your fists were clenched
until you came under the tree.
Oh, but it is still winter this morning, still
and I sit beneath an old mesquite
on a cold concrete bench.
Drops fall into the pond. Blink.
*

Approaching maybe warily
a mother with two small boys in a very large stroller,
a California contraption, stops.
She asks them,
neither old enough to understand
if they hear the drops landing in the pool.

But if any connection is made
between the gentle song
of their mother's trepid voice
and the song of the drops—
the tiniest of communal galaxies
among these choral silences

connected with the intrusion
of my grandmother's fragrance,
her gesture again of sweet acacia,
the breeze through the shade of mesquite
and the soft sound of fountain drops—
it will never be for me to say.

Of course they hear. Each drop is a flute solo.
Each drop is a microphonic concerto.
Each drop is a falling and rising world of choirs
descending in gracefully ascending chords.
Each drop deplores the ritual likelihood
of these children's sacrificial veteran deaths.
     *

Another helicopter,

Sorgmantel

monstrous green cliché of dragonfly
stripped of all shine, all glow, all colors of joy
and any disruption of soul—
for if a dragonfly flies soulless, what does not?—
interrupts.

A basso snarl and rumble.
It is the graceless note,
a Doppler symphony of rude
rising and falling noise, from diminuendo to death.
out of place and time
out of any bounds of nature.

The television flicks back on inside my head.
Blind pixels make themselves heard, felt.
The news throbs its fearful threats of dire security.
But still, the sound of water—
quieter, softer, more nearly pure—
outplays the nattering of the television mind.

Or nearly.
Or nearly.
Blink
blink
blink
blink.
   *

More helicopters.
Our desert garden enters the dank hyper-oxygenated

carboniferous age of the original dragonfly,
the demon-fly of primal jungle,
soggy and explosive at one time.
Foggy Bottom on napalm injections.

Helicopters fumble over us more
often these days than before.
Their peace roars to signal at me
the vast and airy perils
they would protect me from
to the near-end of my days.
*

The bright orange Flame Skimmer will not remember
the diet she inherits from evolution.
She does not need to know
the word for her meal.
She has evolved to nibble out
bits of what we fail to call future.
*

And the mother and the two little boys?—
Choppers above nibble them
gently from the stroller, from the garden.
Like all of us?
Of course—
protect us from . . .
*

Sorgmantel

2. January 2016

... from anything.
Blink
blink
blink
blink.
"Don't move!"
    *

Our hired sailboat glides in white submissiveness
by the rock-strewn wreck
that disguises the Navy's submarine dry-dock.
We bow our heads, not in homage
but to soothe the inner and guilty temptations
of our touristical curiosity.

We salute without motion the megalodon subterfuge
whose primary force on behalf of the nation's security
is the escort police's confiscation of tourist cameras.
We confiscate our own cameras.
Lock up our cameras with our consciences.
We display the instincts of food.

Might it be more seemly for all of us,
even the less than worthy among us
like me, if the helicopters might land and sit quietly,
perch, rest hidden upon the dark greeny bough
of some ancient araucaria,
protect us, me, thereby from themselves?
    *

3. August 1961

Before we embarked for a harbor tour
several wars and a half century ago
my inquisitive touring father
asked a Navy officer, "What's
all that stuff under the tarp
on the ship over there?"

The young officer smiled lieutenantly.
He responded in an official tone,
a well-armed docent,
not unfriendly, not unthreatening
"That is stuff under a tarp"—
"Sir."

The officer smiled then, satisfied.
My father deigned not to peek beneath the official humor.
Blink
blink
blink.
"Don't move!"
    *

Sorgmantel

4. November 2016

Now what exists of our nation—
that which is not stuff under a tarp,
a very big and very thick and incendiary canvas?
One finger on the Tweeter button,
one finger on the red button,
our newly elected prepares to play the world

like a playroom full of slot-cars,
bathtub battleships, model airplanes, toy tanks, lead soldiers—
a small child's elfin trigger finger
and tiny plastic populations poised for melting.
Polaris missiles threaten
to erupt from among innocent bubbles in his tub.

"Don't move!"
    *

  O, Mighty, hear our Public Prayer:
  Allow us to protect ourselves instead O Lord of Hosts
  from all the Hosts that contend to protect us.
  Go all ye quietly out together and let us close the door.
  Amen?
Amen.
    *

5.

Meganeura evolves again.
Lifts off from Carbonifierous
limestone strata.
To my shade for a moment
and just for the moment she is gray.
Let me liven her,

green her world,
gild her,
call her Megan.
Gentle Megan flutters
goldly through her green
swampy life-gorged retreats,

through the ancient dawn again
to the place of hunting.
Midges are large and succulent.
She unfolds her two-foot wingspread.
She dives. Not at me. Not at Us. No me,
not a single Us has lived these peaceful eons past.

Blink.

Blink

. . .

Sorgmantel

Poem in Three Places at Once
after Du Fu and two fellow poets

1. in the manner of David Hinton

Jack pine chill shivers through our north window.
Shards of moonlight shimmer a broad trail
on the lake. A light of settling dew dances slowly.
Stars and clouds ebb and flow in a higher dance.

A small fish flits in the light, almost soundless.
Discussing migration, two loons coo at each other.
Our lives pass between bullets and bellowing.
I am done with keening: night passes over us.

2. *in the manner of David Young*

Red pines sough in the night chill
perplexing the surface of sleep

the moon above our lake
shines a twinkling hedgerow

of unfiltered atoms, silent light
painting a smooth invitation of glow

stars clustered among stray clouds
ebb and flow like early autumn dawns

two loons outside lake-glow
coo to each other about migrating

and the tiny music of a small fish
flipping on the surface of the lake—

far outside the ammo-racket of civil mayhem
and the dis-civil ranting of demagogues

I rise in some quiet hunger outside aliment
moon-glow glides toward us and fades

Sorgmantel

3. RFS, alone with Du Fu

Night-chill shivers off moon-lit cholla,
ghost shadows make un-substance of sleep.

A full moon veils heavy doubt behind
cirrus clouds that heighten the firmament
of doubt. Moonlight is noisier than the hope
of a quail-note some future dawn ago.

Beyond the moon a soul-song of coyotes
shines in the specter-glow of cactus spines.

Somewhere in a pre-dawn pond a desert
pupfish ripples the surface with a dorsal fin
in a shine and silence that mutes the sound and fury
of sheriffs and politicians and vigilante thugs.

I stir in a thirst beyond water-lack. Fierce
cactus spines pretend to soften, protect my
wayward drift into ebbing moon-glow.

In Silence

> *"After Sandy Hook, more than 400 people*
> *have been shot in more than 200 school shootings."*
> New York Times, *February 15, 2018*

How quiet the anguish of surviving now,
gentle murmuring of the young living only a shade
above the silence they grieve, a ticking and a sighing
of bereaved consonants and vowels, lonely

on television only a few feet from my ears. I can't hear
what any words are that might break this quiet
into the treacherous meanings of language.
Can they hear any words themselves, and does it matter?
*

The president stares into his twittering machine,
waiting for a chance to comfort, himself most likely
to be a star if not a king. He recommends arming
teachers—add straw to the murderous pyre.
*

I hear my grandfather's voice again, whose sounds
I haven't heard for half a century, some of it still lonely.
"Hold your mouth right," he jokes again, his voice . . .
sounds I still long for in eternities like this.

His words meant nothing, almost, but the sounds
still say without saying, "I'm here for you.

Sorgmantel

I always will be." I would share the meaning
with these young people, broken-hearted, comforting

one another, and me. But I'll shut up, lest the words
interfere with care. Today, this hour, words are only
noise—I a witness, all I can be, in gratuitous verse.
They whisper to one another. Some touch lightly,

necessarily, say to each other in sounds before
and beyond the bounds of attention, "I'm here for you.
I always will be." Sometimes, we cannot help it,
we hold our mouths right, and we hold together.

We Shall See in Repair the Roads to Our Future

Where shall we find a secure bridge?
Where shall we find a bridge so secure that we can drive over it
and not be distracted

by the knapped shine of the dark river below,
the river we cannot see through concrete rails but which we
                might see
if we dare stop the car

and look down through the broken concrete of our surfaces.
We might see the river between ledges of concrete
framed by rusting rebar.

But we will not stop.
We may be followed tonight.
We have been followed all day so far and so far.

Ah, well.
We know that we will be followed tonight
and that we will still and ever be followed.

Followed.
Followed, we drive.
We drive only as fast as our cracking surfaces allow us.

We drive steady.
We will leave the bridge in time maybe
to leave the car and walk below—

Sorgmantel

beneath the bridge where we may be secure.
In our breath of security we will lie beneath the bridge.
Before we sleep we will look up into the stars

framed by the rotting concrete and rusting rebar
and we will pray to dream that we do not see the surface
begin to crumble down,

begin to be trampled
by the machines and boots that will in-
augurate the heartbeat and throb of our new security.

III. Lyric, Epic, Hearth

en-Chant-ment
An Essay in Three Movements

 . . .

When you heard the still small voice
it wasn't a god you heard.
It was yourself.
It wasn't a god you heard, small, insignificant, powerless.

It was yourself, small, insignificant, powerless.
It was the voice of the silent passing wing.
Yourself.

Listen.
Not too hard.
Ah, not yet

I   Lyric/Epic

Literary characters, if real enough, animating
enter the imagination and memory
with energy to compete with the memories of our own past
family and friends

and even our own past selves
to bring to us a mould and mortal breath.
Eumaeus redirects his attention to converse with my
           grandfather

and I am allowed into the conversation, even
to help direct it on those occasions when they allow
that I am old enough now,
"all bigger" now and only for now:

Sorgmantel

Wealtheow has learned—
taught herself within herself,
which is the only academy for a woman of her status—
that the only way to be in charge is never to need to be in
                charge.
It is a lesson she needn't teach the men.

What is the virtue of listening to anyone in the throes
of the illusion of power,
warrior to berserker in a swig and an insult
and back to sanity through her unnoticed gesture?

Eurydice alive
Orpheus cannot contemplate death.

Without the contemplation of death
the necessary urgency of poetry,

en-chant-ment,
remains still-born.

And poetry with it.

Sorgmantel

The great emotions are lacerating.
We want to demand of the epic that it tether the emotions so
that we can ride them like ponies.

I am looking at the wound
sometimes from the inside
and I want my work to let out the new wild.

Grab the aurochs by the horns and ride.
You.
The past is no more than the past.

The poet only writes.
You ride.
The old poet longs to ride, composes shadows
of horse and rider.

Riding out in the calm, when you hear the still small voice
it isn't a god you hear.
It is yourself.
It isn't a god you hear, small, insignificant, powerless.

It is yourself, small, insignificant, powerless.
It is the voice of the silent passing wing.

A passing owl perhaps
in silent flight through a distant wood
where you are standing.

Yourself.

Listen.
Not too hard, not yet.

. . . the poet's traditional living between
the shaman and the scientist
participating at the extremes as intermediary and as
interlocutor.

The living demands the natural
which attempts to unite the extremes—
which are not really extremes anyway

but life between the inhalations and the exhalations,
the verbs that give threat to the long-held breath.

Sorgmantel

II   Epic/Hearth

It is hard to get lost trying to get lost
because of the efforts of observing, the need
to discover what is strange—lost—
the necessary landscape of lostness.

We strive for the end of our work and our words—
the embodied silence
from which another might create new noises

almost all our own.
And from which the next noises
become words and the next speaker's silence.

When I close my eyes I am expecting
or at least hoping
in some trepidation

for a nuclear light-show glittering about in the vast
and barely visited empyrean
between my ears.

On People Who Are Not:

... names I will have to look up again, and again
and again—
names I will forget again in order to rediscover
the honor of finding them once more—

and to remember the nature of my own names
one honored by Homer who then kindly forgets—
symbol of my own stature with

Tranströmer's Ileborgh, Mayone, Dauthendy, Kaminsky and
in the inevitable rest after the final line of the codex
Tomas as well.
I shall miss them.
I will be them.

Sorgmantel

Nor do you know
through the expected welter of heroic mayhem
the Wealtheow who has learned—
taught herself within herself,

which is the only academy for a woman of her status—
that the only way to be in charge is never to need to be in
        charge.

Wealtheow steps again toward the end of her work and her
        words—
the embodied silence from which she will create *níwe sangas*.
New cantos almost all her own

from which composition of noises come words
that serve to define the necessary
tradition of gesture.

For when she hears the still small voice
it isn't a god she hears.
It is herself.

It isn't a god she hears, small, insignificant, powerless.
It is herself, small, insignificant, powerless.
It is the voice of the silent passing wing.

A silent owl perhaps
passing among the rafters of Heorot.
Herself.

She listens.
Regards the necessary silence.

III   Hearth/Lyric

Notes for the Fenton family:

It is hard to get lost trying to get lost
because of the efforts of observing, the need
to discover what is strange in
the beckoning landscape of lostness.

We strive for clarity in the end of our work and our words—
the embodied silence
from which another might create new clarity

*almos*t all our own.
And from which the next noises
become words and the next storyteller's creative silence

. . . but life is difficult almost always
and life is always as confusing
as life needs to be for what is almost clarity.

Sorgmantel

Hugh Fenton's Story:
    (a theory of fiction)

So. When Hugh hears the Minnie ball whiz by again
you hear it whiz by.
The bee that scared you when you were three.
Or the cannon ball.
You couldn't see it bounce
one two three.

But you could and you did
and it hit you square in the sternum . . .
like when you and your bike fell and the end of the handlebar
hit you square in the sternum.

You've heard them both now
and you have felt the terrible blows
and you can hear now what it is to be scared
and scared near to death.

The irony about speaking of war
is that there is no irony available in speaking of war.
War is too reptilian to be ironic.

Peace is the playground of irony
which happens after the blood has petrified
into the innocent sentimentality of *Epic*

after the poet has dared to return to the people of the hearth—
the warmth of creative peace that is expected to demand
again the hearth-rending culture of war, because

the great emotions are lacerating.
We want to demand of the epic that it tether the emotions so
that we can ride them like ponies.

I am looking at the wound
sometimes from the inside
and I want my work to let out the new wild.

Grab the aurochs by the horns and ride.
You.
The past is so much more than mere time.

The poet writes.
You ride.
We ride.

Sorgmantel

Coda

. . . the poet's traditional living between
the shaman and the scientist
participating at the extremes as intermediary and as
                interlocutor.

The living demands the natural
which attempts to unite the extremes—
which are not really extremes anyway

but life between the inhalations and the exhalations
the verbs that give resonance to the long-held breath.

For when we hear the still small voice
it isn't a god we hear.
It is ourselves.
It isn't a god we hear, small, insignificant, powerless.

It is ourselves, small, insignificant, powerless.
It is the voice of the silent passing wing.
It is Everyvoice in our chorus of mortal breath.

Listen again:

Eurydice alive
Orpheus cannot contemplate death.

Without the contemplation of death
the necessary urgency of poetry,

enchantment,
remains still-born.

And poetry with it.

Sorgmantel

IV. Verse and Reversion

The Room Where We Three Pass
"What a good haunter I am, O tell him"

1
What shall we discover
if we delve
toward the dark lament in the cat

and what feline passion
should try to relieve
from the broken-loved poet

his grieved confusion
at the love
and first despair of his life

his wife
who in dying returned
as specter and muse

loved
unloved
loved and feared for one and twenty fatey verses?

2
I might have stayed longer
to continue some conversation
but the company was no more than

3
I and, ah ...
someone had turned
off the coffee pot

the coffee lying thick in the bottom
of the black mug as moon-dead
as the heart of the cat.

Sorgmantel

Mason Jar

When I opened the big cupboard in the basement where
      my mother stored her plans for that summer's canning
      I saw a single Mason jar.
It was a big jar.
And the old zinc lid was a pewter shade that looked galvanized.
It was dusty.
The whole cupboard was dusty.

When I opened the big cupboard in the basement where
      my mother stored her plans for that summer's canning
      I saw a single Mason jar.
It was a big jar.
A quart jar and I thought I could see the red of tomatoes through
      the untouched dust.
And the old zinc lid was the same pewter shade and the same
      galvanized patina.
It was dustier than before.
The whole cupboard was dustier than before.

When I opened the big cupboard in the basement where
      my mother stored her plans for that summer's canning
      to look again at a single Mason jar
I saw that someone had taken the Mason jar.
It had been a big jar.
It had been a quart jar but I knew that I had not seen the red
      of tomatoes through the untouched dust.
It had been too dusty to see into then.

It should have been dustier now than it had been last time
    I looked.
The galvanized pewter-colored zinc lid was gone too.
The whole cupboard was carpeted in dust.

When I opened the big cupboard in the basement where
    my mother stored her plans for that summer's canning
    I saw that someone had taken the cupboard.
Someone had taken my mother.
But when I opened my hand I could still see my mother's plans
    for this summer's canning.
Then I poured the dust out of my hand and I went back up
    the basement stair.
I turned the key in the ignition of my car.

When I turned round in order to back out the drive onto Rice
    Street I looked at the faces of my granddaughters.
For only a moment their faces were dust too.
Then they were faces again.
They asked why my own face looked so strange.
I did not speak through the dust.

I turned back and drove down Rice Street.
I wanted to show them the old beach on the riverbank where I
    had learned to swim.
I looked out at the river and looking washed off some of the dust.
But I still don't want my granddaughters to see my face.
Not until the dust has dried.
And settled into the patina of my face.
A single Mason jar.
The lid is zinc and it looks like patina of galvanized pewter.

Sorgmantel

Fenton's Lucretius

I
(2018)

After so long and in such longing

Francis Fenton stands at the brim and brew
of Devil's Kettle Falls and
in this spray and foam of dream

pours from a cloudy glass vial an ounce or two
of water from the river named for some tale of Francis'
craft and shady artifice, Fenton River—

Clinamen I: If It Seems Random, It . . .

> *Having dedicated whole*
> *to the destruction*
> *you inspire, the*
> *logic will be to go on doing it*
> *doing it. Having proceeded by* [iv]

could've been the lines I had read
just before I turned to the back of the book
and wrote

Here's

on the left bottom of the recto flyleaf
just before my line of notion was interrupted
by lines of pixels. Ah, Destruction!
Industrious microphysics insulted by the evening news!

They are maybe not the same lines,
maybe not the same poem.
But they'll do for inspiration.
They're all I've got for direction.

For we can't always know
what lines will cohere.
We know that lines cohere somehow, perhaps
like the lines that form Venus' Flower Basket
      for Lucretius' pleasure:

Sorgmantel

3

Prolepsis I: Species of Imagination

Lines of spicules form interstices
of a three-dimensional stage
where performers of diverse skills
and diverse parts participate

in a theater that pretends like all theater,
like all play, to conform into a structure
of a stage-set World, beyond pretense
only the captivity of performance

an illusion of productivity.
It is not to think like the sponge
which makes no thought
but to imagine into the soul of the sponge

and imagine inwardly—not lowly—
from the spiculate form that supports the creature
in a diversity of nearly independent microbes
to the solidity of atoms that support the ether,

all of which demands a construction of no thought
but construction nevertheless
complete only as a draft
constantly edited.

Otherwise we'd be not on
any Earth that would be—
not to cohere.
We don't know *what* lines.

4

What did Pound finally declare about the Cantos?
    "i.e. it coheres all right
              even if my notes do not cohere."

But surely not the Cantos.
Maybe what cohere
are the invisible lines
that wave into sound—
word, cognitive language
to cohere in ways that are almost

incoherent to our questing minds
as the moment just preceding
that microbial internal wriggle
that eventually declared itself LIFE.

Because what follows may be about
the ways in which circumstances

        time
        chemistry
        physics
        unidentifiable particles of stardust
        etc—
        multiples of *et cetera* to the final particle before infinite

converge to allow evolution
to wiggle itself
onto the primordial stage

                    Sorgmantel

to allow for my petty ability
to enjoy reading about "Logic"
in the words, perhaps not at random,
of a similarly evolved
collaboration of those circumstances.

5

Francis Fenton:

I shall say here there is no such condition as immortality.

I say this, and I have no evidence.
I have looked. And looked.
And felt, listened, tasted, sniffed out
for the mortal incense of the creative bang.

We squabble
over immortality who
fear the hopeward condition
of mortality—

the conditions placed on the living
among the competition waged
by the helpless participants
in those conditions.

I say it.
There is no such condition as immortality.
It is not true that nature abhors a vacuum.
Nature abhors tautology.

But I who say it am I who say it.
I am here, saying:
If I die into nothingness
I die into a random fiction of my own poor making.

Sorgmantel

6

Clinamen II: ... Isn't

We avoid traps, the jagged rocks
in order to avoid being snapped and bitten and torn.

We accept being snapped and bitten in traps
in order to accept reality

which is partly oh partly
to accept the experience of being snapped and bitten.

Or do we avoid the traps
in order to avoid experience at all?

Which is to accept a single trepid experience
as though there were no other.

Which is to accept no Other:

Like the graceful Other of the prow of a boat:
canoe, sailboat, rowboat, dragon ship.

What other form so descends
from a history unwritten—

controlled only in experience
and memory—experience experienced

that ascends from form to the same form—

the evolution of function and form.

Never static. Never quite changing.
Like the soul. The molecular constancy of water

made to glow in rippled wakes
behind a grace of controlled interference.

Sorgmantel

7

We sense the mortality of things, Francis, Eumaeus and I.
The soft mullein on the lakeshore.
The lakeshore.

The fossilized segment of an ancient
horsetail—an inch and a half in diameter
from a plant that would tower above

the delicate remnant plants
that grow on the lakeshore and by the road
to the mailbox between Carol and me
and the ferns whose ancestors grew

along, among the ancestors
of the horsetails along some lakeshore
and beside carboniferous ferns burned
to put the Iron Age on wheels

so that the sun would not set on the boot-tracks—
the railroads, the implanted colonial capitols,
the mine-fields and mausolea—the willful amnesia
of the Western World.

Prolepsis II: From Null to Nil, but Something

But even having introduced it maybe
we cannot sense the appropriate oblivion.
The simple nullity.

To address nullity is to address
that which is annulled.
And we are non-annulled, dis-obliviated.
Always in the way.

> "nothing
> I have done
>
> is made up of
> nothing
>
> and the diphthong
>
> ae" ᵛ

Aye?

I have no choice.
Sapient, I *must* think that I am
more a cog of Eternity than I am because I AM
in spite of the *minoritas* I know myself to exist among.

Et tu?

Sorgmantel

9

Francis Fenton:

Of Atoms
            . . . and every word . . .

No. No. No.
not what forms the page
and the ink on the page—
well, those too.
But read the page.
Feel the soft breath that exhales
from your effort.

Consider the light
that rises from the snow of the page.
The light
that issues from the sun or the candle,
even the moon in its gray-lit fullness.

Consider even the nature of ideas
that bounce and shimmer between you
and the word on the page and the words
on the page and your eyes, and you:
the brain of you and the brain itself . . .

Prolepsis III: *"Schoenberg's last word was* Harmonious!*"* vi

Is the last-word watchword the signal to watch *from*
as much—more?—as *for*?
I shall, who have advanced the necessity of Story,
save that word for my own final breath—
Then you at the bed will think that
I want my life to be told for posterity.

You will not know that I mean—
what I might want told,
what I might not want told,
is what proceeds from Story.
And that might be silence.

But even silence remains, a word.
Let death stop at a start, microphysics beyond . . .

Our lives tell no story.
Our narratives
are parts and particles of speech
composed into petty exposition.

  non — je ne
laisserai pas
  le néant vii

. . . and consider also
the mere time it took you

Sorgmantel

to read the words on that page.

Time itself is the repository of every atom.

And what else may be coeval?
Time without atoms is bereft of all things:
the atoms and all that atoms compose.

The oblivion that is you is
still minutely finite
until time
composed around atoms runs out.

Time gone, so runs away
the final possibility of your peculiar
terror of death.

Or no.
Our lives offer up the atoms
of story.

Lucretius . . .

II
(c. 1724)

—The water slips, drips into the fast sheen of the falls.
The falls remix Fenton River, drop by molecule
into the Brule River, and then

a vapor of nearly discrete particles
spreads and flows under Lake Superior and into Wisconsin
and follows U.S. Route 2 to near Brule Lake and then, then

becomes a ghost of the vapor of the river itself and Francis
spread wide
to contract again into the original flow

but out of all control save Fenton's wyrd gesture
spread out and in and out and in, undulating
until nowhere is not this river, is not less than anywhere.

Sorgmantel

12

Clinamen III: If It Seems Systematic, It . . .

The meadowlark dead on a country blacktop
is two ways removed from the wreck of Earth.

The bird and our hearing are silenced.
The charm of its small beauty erodes into the ditch.

Out of our natural distances we have much
to offer by way of our misunderstanding:

Misunderstanding the meadowlark
we are always in awe of its beauty

and the joy we misunderstand
to be the bird's joy, not ours—and broken.

Misunderstanding death we remain
in awe of the power we believe

belongs to some force called Death.
How dully fearsome to see death as it is:

the simple molecular change into no-change.
Better for me that I slip into the lake

and feel again over my whole body
the constant change in changeless water.

V. Mourning Cloak II

Sorgmantel
"In the still of the night once again I hold you tight."
"Deep Purple," Peter De Rose, 1933

Gray stucco shudders.
A scrap of dirty gray slips off, flutters
upward in a beauty of grim purple, then

mottled gray again. Then
lands on—what?
What? Reflection jounces with my father's Buick.

Ivy covered walls—outside somewhere among racing cacti.
Mourning purple darkens mourning lilacs instead
and I lean my head against the mourning

evening purple outside the car window.
Back seat, nineteen-fifties Sonoran night.
"Deep Purple."

In that waning mist of memory no "you"
breathes my name yet and I have never yet
sung that stanza's last word but flat.

Mourning will be always sung in choir-perfect key.
Mourning never is.
The purple of it shudders.

Gray again. Concrete under ivy.

Flake of dull ash sways from her lilac blossom.
Then a release again into deep purple, lorn purple.

The butterfly rests on her lilac, sips
and darkens the fragrance of loss.
And I remember.

Memories sung on key are contrived, conventional, choral.
Memory will rise to the well-rim of the mind always off-key.
The sigh rises confused, sorgmantel in dark flutter:

My father mantled at the wheel of his Buick.

Sorgmantel

Common Icons of New England

this is not the place
to consider
the directions
we might or might not
take

this is the place
to look about and consider
the directions we
have been given—
have given—
look up
and down
in and out
of our lives

Sorgmantel

        once
you have found
    the place
the second time
     the third
    will come
or come back
      to you
     and . . .
*   and*

hit the eye like
the hapless language
of our ancient children

Sorgmantel

's headstones

:

et, et, et

Sorgmantel

Transparencies

I
How we hanker for fall
in its browns and yellows and reds,
its industry and fire of dying.

But it is after the color in our walks through
the new gray of the woods that I am granted new vision,
and pause.

It is the transparency those colors reveal slowly
as they become one color with the chill
and drift off into their season of eternity.

It is the clear space, through dark interstices,
the black-widow-future's gentle tangle of web,
the pewter light around the remnant trunks and branches.

It is the hill over there that I have walked on but seen
for the underbrush only in the drear seasons,
when I can exorcise the habit of my care-blindered eyes

scouting for poison ivy or the next mischievous thorn;
I can exorcise even intent,
the delusionary lure of human misdirection.

New transparency opens the forest to the broken trees
lying on the same quiet hill, trunks

all fatally mown in one sarcophagal direction,

facing east these silent years,
toward the lake,
toward the rising ghosts of tomorrow.

2
The trees have lain there
slowly rotting for almost two decades now,
since the two early morning wind-storms

that took a generation of aged aspen,
nurse trees left by lumber barons to care for the shorn forest
with shade and rotting leaves.

The aspen had finished by then their mothering the forest
for the century since the old forest was cleared to free
the cold shining air around this nurturing death.

3
The same transparent fall, the flight of geese
cheered my grandmother in her last calm days,
in perfect health at ninety-two, save that she was dying.

Fall guided my mother too, or its beauty wrested from her
the last great sadness, a life so many years in the ending
that grief had exhausted itself into a silence,

a veil that fell so long before her death
that she could finally die

Sorgmantel

outside the curse of merely spoken love.

4
Fall is our walking to that stand of red pine,
the one that stood at a brush-disguised distance,
as we thought two weeks ago.

Now it is right here where we walk to count
the dead and dying pines, victims of drought and insects,
old age, want and, who knows? Maybe intent.

And the few already on ground
we had never seen before. More intent?
In some ways we are quickened by the quaint ironies of death.

5
We could say a few words over our Earth-clad dead,
but the words are already and always being said, in kinship,
by the clarity of the season.

After Time After

After we have gotten to know each other for a few
more decades
or sometime impossibly geologic maybe

then we can walk together—
look at the colors, shapes, or what is shapeless
to any other creature but still recognizable.

The woods we have gotten to know so well or not so well.
Talk about, perhaps, that showdown
between the fox and the groundhog

and what genius protected the one from the many
or the many from the one, the nature of standoff
that even in the absence of love saves the potential.

Or wonder together why the language of crows
seems so different today when nothing else is different.
Or so we had thought

before the crows thought to remind us
and remind whatever is so silent
down there in Fenton Fen

where we had got used to the spring peepers
peeping in impossible decibels
for love love love

Sorgmantel

and while we let the conversation enter
the common silence we can
start
    *

to gesture toward the shadows looming in our direction.
Take Ithaca, the gesture offers.
Welcome to the next dust
    *

and start to get to know each other as well
here or in Ithaca or, no no no!
Both, neither and therefore when/wherever.

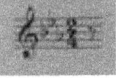

Notes

i Language moves across the complex surface
               of its possibilities
Then falls back
After a brief
consummation

"Sorgmantel" ("Mourning Cloak") from *A Child is not a Knife, Selected Poems of Göran Sonnevi*, trans. and ed. Rika Lesser.

ii Engraving of *Prodryas persephone*, 1887.

iii Gary Snyder's apparent dating system. It is no more accurate than any other, but no less precise, and it avoids the snobbery of culture-bound systems, especially the euphemistic BCE/CE.

iv Alice Notley, "Logic," in *Songs and Stories of the Ghouls*.

v William Carlos Williams, *Spring and All*, vi.

vi Gören Sonevi, *Mozart's Third Brain*, xxxiv.

vii Stephane Mallarmé, "Un Tombeau pour Anatole," 190.

www.ingramcontent.com/pod-product-compliance
Lightning Source LLC
LaVergne TN
LVHW091311080426
835510LV00007B/468